CALLING GOD SHE
?

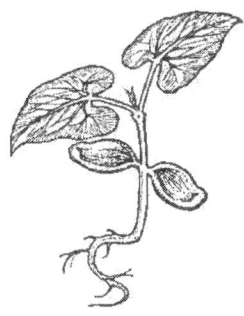

Reflections and Insights
of a great-grandmother,
retired clergywoman,
and doctor of theology

Barbara Thorington Green

Calling God
She
?

**Reflections and Insights
of a great-grandmother,
retired clergywoman,
and doctor of theology**

Copyright © 2014 Barbara Thorington Green. All rights reserved

ISBN-13: **978-1495365898**

No part of this book may be reproduced in any form whatsoever, print or electronic, without written permission, except in the case of brief quotations embodied in critical articles or reviews.

For information regarding rights and permissions, contact

Barbara Thorington Green,

email pb1278@aol.com

204 Allen Rd.
Port Crane, NY 13833

Table of Contents

Preface		Page iv
1.	'She' God?	Page 1
2.	Ideas Sprouting	Page 9
3.	Change?	Page 16
4.	Gender Differences?	Page 20
5.	Where Did I Come From?	Page 26
6.	Generation after Generation	Page 32
7.	Is Today a New Day?	Page 44
8.	Tripping Through My Religious Life	Page 50
9.	Women's Ways?	Page 56
10.	Clergywomen	Page 62
11.	Odes to my Mentors Mary Magdalene - - Simone Weil	Page 71
12.	Visions of God?	Page 84
13.	Messages from God?	Page 90
14.	After-Thoughts	Page 96
Bibliographies		Page 98

PREFACE: WHY I WRITE

We talk about God. We write about God. We use words. Letters, words, and language are all developed constructs. All language falls short of what we perceive as reality. Try answering the question "who are you?" with words. You can't quite catch your essence. Yet words help us communicate with each other. The word 'God' and the language we use for 'God' has come out of thousands of years of patriarchal ages and mindsets with their presuppositions and assumptions.

Many are moving away from patriarchal living and thinking. In nearly all our Christian Churches we continue to use words like *Father, Lord,* and *He* when referring to what we consider the divine reality. Even now, our references to God are usually masculine, reinforcing the assumption that God is male and has male characteristics. This has been a presupposition for most, something we assume and seldom think or talk about.

Recently I have asked myself: ""What about feminine words like *Mother* and *She*? Could these images be used as we consider the Divine?" Our present mostly masculine references to God inevitably encourage women to see themselves as less than men, and inevitably encourage men to see themselves as more than women. As boys and girls hear this limiting language, do they automatically believe likewise? I notice and address this today because our society is moving toward the recognition of the importance of women's voices, work, and lives in the public arena. Women now publicly ask, and even demand, not to be put down as less significant than men.

As mother of women and grandmother of men and observer of life in general, I have noted changes over the years in expectations associated with gender and yet continue to notice confusion regarding many of the old stereotypes regarding importance, power, responsibilities, etc. I hope my great-grandchildren discover a world in which their gender does not determine their importance in either the private or public sphere, or even within themselves.

During my years as pastor and retreat leader I became aware of the pain and suffering many women carry because of the abuse they have experienced in their lives. One woman in her eighties told me she was sexually used as a child and then told it was her fault when she tried to speak of it, so she kept quiet until she shared it with me. I would like to think these things no longer occur but I know otherwise. At meetings, I often note women speak up until a man speaks strongly, and then women tend to be quiet about their opinions and concerns. By continuing to use male language for God without using female language are we complicit in quieting women and are we even complicit in the denigration, use, and abuse of women? In some discussion groups, people bring up female images of God, but I see very little movement to follow up with feminine language for God.

During my years as a student, I had the privilege of reading the works of many medieval religious women and discovered voices speaking of passionate love and life both for and from God. Their writings touched me in ways no other readings had, not even what we call Biblical writings. Some of these religious women would refer to God with a feminine image here and there, but they continued to call God 'He' reflecting the assumption of God's maleness. Writings by Simone Weil and Susanna Wesley increased my awareness that I connect with some women's writings in more significant ways than any writings by men. Eventually my studies turned to the preaching of clergywomen and then studies of what might be called 'women's ways'. I have come to think women have 'ways' that the world needs. This leads me to the question: What if we referred to God as she? How would that affect us, our visions of God, and our realities?

This brief book is written to summarize some of my reflections and insights. It is written to invite the reader to consider the present assumptions of the male nature of God and to consider fuller understandings of God. I believe future references to God in our thoughts, churches, homes, and on the streets, need to include an equal blend of feminine and masculine images and language. It seems to me our present ways of only considering the maleness of God is harmful to both men and women. It may have seemed appropriate in the past, but it is not now and it will not be in the future. We need fuller visions. Some suggest a genderless God, I have tried that for over twenty years without satisfaction. The challenges are great, the needs are immediate. Children are listening.

Practical Points
I write in thought and/or stress lines. This way of writing forces me to be more concise and precise. I hope the style makes my thoughts easier to read and understand. I write briefly to leave room for your life, thoughts, and jottings on each page. I encourage you to freely think and write. The italicized sections tend to be insights and the plain print my reflections.

Each section is included because it suggests questions or topics that played major roles in the development of my present understandings and questions. If you find yourself disinterested in a section, I ask that you skip over it and continue reading. If you find yourself more interested in a section, you can find lists of books at the end to help you find my sources and pursue the topic.

Barbara Thorington Green
2014

1. 'SHE' GOD?

We know the 'He' God.
'He' has gotten all the attention
Could we conceive of a 'She' God?
How can we come to know Her?
Something within me yearns for Her
Yet I cannot imagine it.
I hunger to hear God called 'She'
On the streets, in churches, everywhere.

Male language has been used for 'God'
in our culture for thousands of years.
All language is metaphoric
but over time metaphors take on reality.
Whatever we mean by 'God' is
certainly beyond language.
However, when we hear God called
'He', 'Father', 'Lord'
from birth or before,
we naturally assume
God has a male nature.
We need fuller images of God,
images that intentionally include
female references to God's identity.
Around the world women are
gaining respect and recognition
in the public sphere

as well as the private.
Perhaps it is time to
re-form our images of God,
time to expand God's identity.
In this less patriarchal age
perhaps it is time for our God-talk to reflect
the inclusion of women.
Many societies are moving away from
the assumption of male supremacy
and male dominance.
I believe it is time for us to do likewise
in our God-talk.

I have lived and worked
in the traditions of the past.
From birth I have prayed to a male God,
calling God 'Father'
and referring to God as 'Lord' and 'He'.
I had heard no other language.
I have nearly always attended
(United) Methodist Churches
where worship and discussions
refer to God with words and thoughts
that named God male.
Scriptures assume the masculine identity of God.
the pronoun 'he' is often used for God
but never the pronoun
'she'.
It is time to challenge these outdated
and troubling traditional practices.

I am not male,
I am not masculine.
I am not a he.
My three daughters are not.
Are men more
similar to the divine than we are?
Are women
created in God's image?
Have men created God
in their own image?
This was probably inevitable,
when they had the only public voice.
Now it is different.

Am I bad?
Am I considering something evil?
Will such imaginings be destructive?
-or-
Is it goodness I am reaching for?
Would boys and girls, women and men
be blessed by these considerations.

Can I refer to God as 'She', 'Mother', 'Her'
as often and as easily
as I have referred to God as
'He', 'Father', Lord?
To absorb more truth of God
I need to widen my images of God

to include the female,
not in some minor, superficial way
but in the very core of my being.
Can I?
Can I do it aloud?
In the church? Every day?
It is hard to imagine.

What would 'She' be like?
Would She love to sit and talk,
have a cup of tea in order to come closer?
Would She join in the conversations,
trying to figure out everyday life?
Would She listen and hear?
Would She chit-chat with me?
Would She nurture rather than command?
Would She walk by my side,
be part of my journey?
What does it mean to be a 'she'?
Would She help me figure it out?
Would She shed a tear with me?
Would She appreciate my intuitions?
Would She respect my emotions?
What would it mean to worship 'Her'?
Would visions of 'women' change?
Would girl's self-images expand?
Will the world be different
when God is free to be 'She'?

Daily conversations,
worship gatherings,
scriptures, and
entertainment media
continue to
lead us to conclude that God is male.
Lords are men.
Fathers are men.
The consistent use of
'He' and 'Him' for God,
in homes, on the streets, in media, and in churches,
assumes, and teaches our children to assume,
that God is male.

I excluded 'he' references to God
for many years,
using the term 'God' instead.
Without pronouns
my personal relationship with God
seemed to deteriorate,
and what was left was still masculine.
Some call this inclusive language
I found it excluded all.

Words have power.
With male labels,
God also has been given male characteristics
in the minds of those
who hear, speak, write and/or read.

I expect this begins in utero.
I am very attached to many wonderful men,
but where does this leave women?
For better or for worse,
this automatically identifies men with God
and leaves women as 'something else'.
This pre-birth assumption
automatically elevates men
and denigrates women.
Perhaps both men and women
are tired of this.

Are you hungering to call God 'she'?
I sense that God is hungering to hear it.
You may not have considered it.
You may believe this conversation crosses
an unacceptable line.
You may not even think you want
to approach this subject.
You may be content with the situation as it is.

One of my favorite theologian/philosophers,
Simone Weil, wrote about hunger.
She pointed out
the real danger is not hunger,
but a lack of knowing
we are hungry.
When we know we are hungry,
we search for and cry out for food.
When we don't know, we starve.
Perhaps many are starving to call God 'She'
but the possibility hasn't occurred to them.
They do not know they can.
Can they?

It is hard to imagine people
easily referring to God
with words indicating 'woman'.
It is foreign to my being.
Would it alter expectations
and create a healthier world
for both men and women?
Would it open up new possibilities
for us and for generations to come?
Would our brothers, husbands, sons, and grandsons
benefit?
Would our sisters, wives, daughters, and granddaughters
benefit.

Perhaps it could be like this:
We come to you,
Mother of us all.
Cradle us in your loving arms.
Speak to us with your kind words.
We yearn to know you are near.
Please reach out and touch us.
We need your healing salves.
Sing to us, calm our anxieties,
soothe our fears.
Help us claim ourselves
as your beloved children.
Encourage us to be bold
in our living and our loving.
Give us confidence in our voices.

*Let our words speak what is within us.
We want to know you better
as mother as well as father.
We speak out of the depths of our beings,
beings that were created in your womb.*

2. NEW IDEAS SPROUTING

A seed planted
Buried in the soil
For a day, a week, a month, a year, a decade
Germination
Life appears imminent
Moisture and warmth
Fertilizer helps
A sprout
Just a beginning
A showing of life
Maneuvering around stones and obstacles
Pale and anemic
Growth without light
Yet toward the light
Until it reaches the surface.

Then color appears
The sprout shoots upward
But now danger lurks
It may be eaten by a foraging animal
It may drown in a downpour
It may burn up in a drought
Someone may pull it for a weed
Or a tasty snack.
Sometimes the seed becomes a mighty oak
An apple tree
A dandelion
A radish.
Something to relish or something to consume
-or-
Something to toss out.

*Too many times we toss out what we should relish
And relish what needs to be tossed out
And far too often we consume it all
And turn it into fertilizer for another day.*

*It is hard to decide when it is just starting its life.
Ideas are like this.
Some we need to nurture
For our good and the good of the world.*

About three years ago,
I spouted off to a very gentle pleasant
Staff Parish Relations committee member
"I just have to call God 'She'!"
I was quick to apologize
and move the conversation to something else.
The person was kind enough
not to bring the brief emotional explosion
of his clergywoman to the full committee.
Of course, I had been thinking about it, but
why was there so much angry passion
in my declaration?

Shortly after that,
I met a clergywoman I was mentoring for lunch.
We were to have some appointed conversation.
A clergyman sat down with us.
We welcomed him
and continued the conversation.
I was moving us toward a discussion

of using non-gendered language for God.
After some conversation had elapsed,
the clergyman said that he frequently
found himself using 'He" for God out of habit.
He didn't really mean anything by it.
Something inside me rose up.
I replied caustically:
"If I can refrain from calling God 'She',
you can refrain from calling God 'He'!"
Where did the acid in my voice come from?

I had never considered myself
radical or feminist.
Those words seemed 'bad' to me,
but I was becoming consumed
with a question:
Is half of God's image missing?
Missing from our daily conversations,
missing from our worship dialogue,
missing from our scriptures,
missing from our tradition,
missing from our lives?
Missing

After eagerly and joyously leading worship
for nearly twenty years,
I could no longer stand
in front of men, women, boys, and girls
and say "Our Father . . ." without feeling uneasy.
I could no longer sing the old familiar hymns

without being struck with the strong focus
on the maleness of God.
I could no longer lead in what I had come to see
as a religious system that
covertly and overtly
elevated the male over the female.
I could no longer lend my voice
to what I have come to see
as the oppression of women
in a system that declares freedom from oppression
in its baptismal vows.

How could I go from dedicating my life to church
to challenging this very basic understanding?
This would have seemed
foreign and irrational
only a few years ago.
The question continued:
How could I, a woman,
lead a congregation of boys and girls,
men and women,
with language and stories that uncritically
come out of the assumptions of a different time,
a time that assumed
the higher value of men than women?
Was I putting my stamp of approval
on this assumption?
Would direct conversation about this
alienate people?
Changing 'Lord' and 'he' to 'God'
didn't help.
People seldom picked up the practice.
Even if they did,
there is more to this discussion
than changing

'He' language
to 'God' language.

Years before, I was in a weekly lectionary group.
The topic turned to using the
scriptural and traditional word 'men' for people.
My non-thinking flip comment was:
"it doesn't bother me,
I feel included in the term 'men'".
One of them looked at me.
I can recall his words verbatim:
"Barbara, I have never once
thought of you as a man."
At the time, I was jolted;
of course I didn't want them
to think of me as a man.
I just wanted to get along, be part of the group.
I loved the church and its ways.
The fuller reality of his comment
took years to incubate.

I became bolder as I met with clergywomen.
Behind closed doors,
I would occasionally remove masculine pronouns
and insert the feminine,
a 'she' for a 'he', a 'her' for a 'him'.
Once in a while another of the women would.
It felt so good.
I can't begin to tell you
the extent of the gift of those moments.

I was in a warm bath.
One clergywoman said even her posture tended to change
into a more relaxed mode
whenever we gave ourselves this freedom.
This seemed to be the balm in Gilead
we had all sung about.
It always led to new insights, and thoughts.
I worried we were doing something 'wrong',
but it felt just the opposite.
It seemed to me, we were speaking
according to God's will and not against it.
I looked forward to those moments;
but were they damaging for clergywomen
who had many years to work in traditional congregations?
Why did it feel so good?
What difference does it really make?

I shared some writings recently.
They referred to God as 'she'.
I received this reply
"Your poetry helps,
just hearing the 'She' heals.
I'm always startled by how much
hurt there is in the constant 'he-s',
I don't notice until they are absent."
She named it so well.
It is easy to not recognize
the situation for what it is.
For more than sixty years I had not noticed.
Yet now I become ill at ease and even angry
with every 'He', 'Lord', 'Father'
reference to God.

The summer before I retired
I sat with others at a picnic table.
People were inquiring about my future plans.
I decided to risk being honest.
I told them I felt I had to examine this desire
to call God 'She'.
I expressed my concern that
women were not encouraged to take
themselves or their abilities seriously
with our present ways of speaking of God.
To my surprise the Jewish woman on my left said
they already had a group that was often saying:
"My God, She wouldn't do that!"
I could tell I had struck a chord
with the active Roman Catholic
intelligent and capable woman on my right.
I saw her wipe away a tear.
No one around the table
seemed to question the idea or the need.
They didn't even seem shocked!
Perhaps many are ready for this conversation.
Perhaps many want someone to speak.
How many are ready
and eager
for changes?

3. CHANGE?

Change comes.
Every morning a new day,
the same sun, but . . .
Every month, a new cycle,
the same moon, but . .
Every generation, new life,
every infant, new possibilities.
There are similarities,
yet there are changes.
It can't be stopped.
Sometimes we welcome newness.
Sometimes we brake as hard as we can.
Stopping change robs us.
We remain prisoners of the past.
Some changes just happen,
sometimes we have a say.
Often it's a mixture of the two.
Expectations for women and
expectations for men
have changed with the times.
We forget the change has even happened
after twenty years or so.
But in the moment
change can seem monumental

The world is rapidly changing.
Women are entering every career
and field of employment.
Women are graduating with bachelor degrees,
master degrees, and PhDs
in numbers often equal to
or greater than men.
Women are moving away
from being seen as subsidiaries
and second-class citizens.
More and more frequently
women are publicly leading,
and they are beginning to lead
in their own styles
rather than imitating the
male-oriented styles of the past.

Women are now freer
to use their voices, talents, and abilities
in the public sphere.
Are women and men finding previous
images of God
restrictive or even irrelevant?
As women become
more respectful of themselves and other women,
will they, too, come to feel that
the puzzle pieces no longer fit,
that something is wrong with the assumptions.
Will others find it natural and helpful
to include a 'she' God?
Is this an option?

Are we free to find new images of God?
Not just in the fringes,
but in the mainline?
Are we free to explore and investigate?

Are we free to call God 'She'?
Can we imagine hearing God called 'She'?
In everyday conversation?
In public broadcasting?
In church?
In scriptures?
In prayers?

I find it harder than I would expect,
even in my private spiritual life.
I have had a lifelong relationship with God,
a God named with male language
and given male characteristics.
I have loved
a male and masculine God.
I have difficulty freeing myself for more,
but I remember the goodness of
the times I heard God called 'She'.
I believe more complete images of God
are critically important
for women and men
for girls and boys.

Can we think this?
Can we say this?
Can we hear this?
Can we read this?
:

O give thanks to God
For She is good
Her steadfast love endures for ever
O give thanks to the God of gods,
For her steadfast love endures forever.

???????

For thousands of years
we have said:

O give thanks to God
For He is good
His steadfast love endures for ever
O give thanks to the God of gods,
For his steadfast love endures forever.

Why does the 'she' seem
so strange yet so attractive?

4. GENDER DIFFERENCES?

*What does it mean
To say I am a woman?
Who are women?
Who are men?
Is it different in every situation?
Is it different in every age?
Are there generalities to be noted?
In Eden, 'Woman' seems to be
an afterthought, an 'other',
an aide, a companion for man.
But there is the other Biblical story
in which woman is created
in God's image.
What are we to believe?
What are we to live by?
If I am created in God's image,
then woman must resemble God.
How can that be?
I have (almost) always called God
Father, Lord, He.
A woman has never been a Father.
A woman has never been a Lord.
A woman has never been a 'he'.*

*Does this conversation matter?
Are women's voices different?
Are women's actions different?
Are women's thoughts different?
Are women's assumptions different?
Do women see the world through different lenses?
Women are different one from another,
can we generalize some similarities?*

Let's think about some everyday events.

When my husband, Paul, is out of town,
I watch the television shows that annoy him.
When I am out of town
he watches the shows that annoy me.
He likes a clear-cut image of the 'bad'.
He likes to see badness destroyed;
fists, guns, knives, bombs, whatever it takes.
He assumes this is the 'best' way.
I like relational shows
where 'bad' is less prominent, perhaps grayer,
and through conversations and interactions,
something more 'good' comes about.
I assume this is the 'best' way.
I guess the goal is the same –
to make the world a better place,
but the shows are very different.
The ways of proceeding are nearly opposite.
I am sure this is not universal but
many of my friends report similar experiences.

Paul reads Westerns.
Sometimes he picks up one written by a woman,
I hear grunts and groans throughout his reading.
Either she gives too much detail

or goes on about a romantic relationship.
I prefer to read autobiographies.
When they are written by men
I note a confident "I-ism" that leads me to admire them
and see their goodness.
When they are written by women
I note a less-strident 'we-ism'
that leads me to connect with them and their complex lives.
To me, women's writings present a more real picture of life.
There is more chaos.
There is less assertion of rightness.
Relationships have importance,
Feelings and emotions are included.
The women more often invite me in
whether or not they solve problems.

Many have studied gender differences.
Their studies have led television shows,
advertisers, publishers, and speakers
to consider the gender of their audiences.
Gender differences are seldom concrete,
there are always exceptions.
(Are differences biologically
or socially constructed?)
There is a chromosome difference.
Women and men have hormonal differences.
Some scientists suggest differences
in men's and women's brains.
Often girls and boys have differing expectations
placed before them.
Expectations have power.

We raised three daughters,
then we watched each daughter raise two sons.
There were inherent differences
in the activities and attitudes
between the genders.
I taught nursery school for many years.
I observed different
behaviors and activity preferences
between boys and girls,
with few exceptions.

We attend our grandson's football games.
I notice most women cheering
for good plays and ignoring minor errors.
I notice most men verbally noting the mistakes
and errors on the part of
players, coaches, and referees
and ignoring minor successes.

If my father had written our family history
It would be very different than my mother's.
If my husband wrote our family history
It would be very different than mine.
We remember different events,
We interpret them differently.

The timelines might be similar but
my mother and I
would include more of our feelings,
more of our private thoughts,
more of the day to day.

On and on.

If we give credence to gender difference,
we must consider what this means for churches
and religious thought.
They have been structured and developed by men
for thousands of years.
Now women are frequently leading
in religious systems designed by men;
preaching from scriptures written by and for men.
Are clergywomen even aware?
Do we notice a misfit?
Do we sometimes think things just don't add up?
Do we feel like a puzzle piece being
pressed into a puzzle not created by or for us?
We can't go backwards,
if we are going to address this issue,
it has to be now and in the future.
If our scriptures were written by men,
where are we going to find women's words
and women's thoughts to ground our faith in?
If our language for God developed
in a society
that assumed the greater significance of men,

how are we going to create appropriate spiritual/religious
language and metaphors for God today?
How are we going to describe
the One we praise and turn to for help?
What are we going to call the source of our being?
Is the elimination of any gendered language the answer?
Or is the inclusion of feminine images
at every occasion the better answer?

Can we say it?

God created humankind
in her image
In the image of God
she created them
Male and female,
she created them ????

For thousands of years
We have assumed God's 'he-ness'
Can we accommodate an addition?

5. WHERE DID I COME FROM?

Me
A girl who liked to think and ponder
looking in the stream and sky.
A curl in the middle of my forehead
When I was good...And when I was bad...
A pretend friend named Beedsie-Bideso
kept me company.
I giggled with my younger sister.
I grew tall
and was able
to do many things-
I cared for my baby brother.
I never needed a doll,
I changed real diapers
and cuddled a real child.
I weeded the garden.
I made most of my clothes.
I helped lay floor tile.
I carried milk
and moved bales.
I dusted and mopped.
I set tables.
I cooked and baked.
I climbed trees, I laid in meadows.
I loved puzzles of every kind.
Most of my life,
I have thought it 'preferable' to do 'guy things'
than 'girl things'.
Frequently my mother cared for my cousins.
The older ones were boys
and my older sibling was a boy

*I played with them,
I built with blocks
and ran toy cars.
I enjoyed being with them,
it was exciting and fun.*

I grew up on a hundred-cow dairy farm
six miles out of town.
We were the only inhabitants of our dead-end road.
Girlfriends my own age didn't 'happen'.
At school I was often chosen early in the
kickball picks.
I felt important and better than
girls who went off to swing.
From my earliest memories I felt important
because I could keep up with the guys.
They looked out for me
and made me feel special.

I learned of women's roles and ways of being.
They were different than men's.
I overheard many conversations.
Women were not supposed to work
outside the home
if their husbands could provide.
If they were employed, women should be
secretaries, nurses, and teachers
but certainly not
doctors, ministers, or principals.
My aptitude tests came back

suggesting I should be an engineer.
Much laughter ensued in the classroom.
Of course, I didn't want to be an engineer!
I never remember wishing to be a boy but
I certainly had higher opinions of boys than girls.
I expected to become a missionary doctor.
That would be acceptable.

My mother tried to turn down
a nomination for the school board
because that would be 'up to my father'.

While we were always in Sunday School,
we almost never attended worship services
because Dad was unable to accompany us
due to his farm schedule.
People might 'talk' if we attended without him.

My father's work seemed much more
exciting and important
than mopping the floors,
canning vegetables,
or setting the table.
My brothers knew how to dust and mop,
but they were expected to help with farm chores
and I think they preferred it.

I knew how to carry milk and get the cows,
but I was expected to help my mother,
did I prefer it?
Mom was appreciative and praised me frequently.
I loved praise.

'Father Knows Best' was a favorite TV show.
I believed the title defined what was proper.
My father was quietly kind, hard-working,
and deep thinking.
My mother appeared to make the decisions
and be in control.
Mother had a business degree,
my father left school in the 11th grade
to support himself.

My maternal grandmother had been a teacher,
and all of her sisters educated.
Many strong women were part of my life.
Men were to be the in-charge strong ones.
Often it seemed the women tried
to make them feel they were.
When a man asserted an opinion
the women usually fell silent.

Sunday School was very important in my life.
I attended the nursery class,
where my mother taught, even before I was born.
Sunday School teachers were all women.
However, the really important ones:
God, Jesus, and our clergy
were obviously male.
I learned the stories well.
I could answer every question.
I began to memorize the Bible.
I was always interested and able.
I guess I was always religious,
or at least eager to please
and to be recognized.

I became an adult.
I definitely had the passionate feelings of a girl.
I married right out of high school.
Our children arrived.
I began to teach Church School
and served the church in many capacities.
I grew in my faith.
I was usually good at what I did
and I did my best to be a 'good' wife and mother,
waiting on my husband,
doing everything I could for everyone,
trying to restrain my own desires –

Of course God was male
and masculine,

in charge,
powerful,
unchanging,
knowing everything.
Father God, like Father, knew best.
The Bible told me so.
The hymns that I sang over and over
told me so.
The preachers told me so.
The women teachers told me so.
I would never have imagined it otherwise.

Could there have been another thought to add:
Mother God, like Mother, knew best?
I never saw that show
-or-
sang that song.

6. GENERATION AFTER GENERATION

We come and we go
Embryos,
Infants,
Girls and boys,
Youths,
Young adults
Middle-aged
Elderly
At some point, deceased.
The new becomes old
The once 'never was' ceases to exist.
Each has a moment to live and to be.

Changes come
With every generation.
New ideas
New ways
Born
Grow
Live
Die.
Newness comes
It becomes old
Every generation reshapes the world.
The world reshapes every generation.
Molding and remolding
Who we will be is never established.

My great-grandmother
sat in a rocker and did needle work.
Her life dependent on son and daughter-in-law
in Grand Gorge, NY
My maternal grandmother
canned and baked bread,
milked cows,
read magazines,
washed their few clothes on Monday.
Tuesdays irons sat on the wood stove.
She rested her rheumatic heart.
Reclusive with one neighborhood friend,
she seldom went to town.
She taught for a while in a one room schoolhouse,
going to school by horse and wagon.
When they got a car,
it seldom went more than a few miles.
She never drove.
Grand Gorge, NY

My paternal grandmother
was seldom mentioned –
A milliner who travelled to NYC
in her early life,
she 'ran off' leaving husband and six children.
She worked on women's suffrage.
Eccentric?
She drove,
her car travelled fast.
Her letters filled with bits of scripture,
came in used envelopes steamed
and turned inside out.
????

My mother – always hard working
Cooked and washed for eight or ten or twelve.
Gardens of vegetables, rhubarb and berries fed us.
She cleaned and cooked for 'summer people'.
She carried milk in the barn.
Piles of laundry on Mondays,
meant wringer washer and tubs of rinse water,
and lines full of clothes.
Then – later an iron that plugged in,
an electric washer and dryer
"I'd give up my washer before my dryer"
How she hated frozen jeans!
A poetic writer,
she found time for lengthy letters.
Doors were always open for
frequent family visitors.
There were long phone calls with friends.
She loved her home and her 'in town' jobs.
She loved contacts with others.
She drove up to 50 miles on occasion.
She lived busily until age 54.
Died of cancer
Grand Gorge, NY

Myself – always restless
Busy at one thing or another
Wife, daughter, mother, sister, friend,
stay at home Mom, volunteer,
nursery school teacher, mail carrier,
medical office assistant, pastor, student,
(doctor of theology at age 59),
always thinking and puzzling.
I have tried to care for family needs
and pay some attention to my own.
I drove around the eastern half of the country to interview
clergywomen
and frequently the 300 miles to Boston and back.
I served large and small churches.
I came to know people around the country
through church and academia as well as family.

Port Crane, NY
Three daughters

The oldest –Patty - single mother of two young men
Grandmother of an amazing little boy
and precious twin girls.
Systems Analyst for a grain company
Sees possibilities and makes them happen
Quilter
House renovator
Lover of fun
Always able
As a young woman
She put her family and all belongings in a huge
U-Haul truck and drove to Kansas.
Now in Enid, Oklahoma

Stephanie – married mother of two young men
Special education teacher
Compassion and care for all
Farmer and gardener
Many gather in her home
Known for her upbeat attitudes
4-H leader
Can hook up the largest of full cattle trailers
and drive off to auctions by herself.
Garden Plain, Kansas

Michelle – married mother of two teen boys
Hard-working, award-wining merchandizer
Often drives 150 miles a day for work
Loves vacations
Great hostess and home decorator
Everyone loves her parties
Marathon runner
Always in training – with friends
Enjoys looking attractive and stylish
Fun-loving and joy-filled.
Binghamton, NY

All our daughters are in frequent touch with
numerous people:
family, classmates, friends from past and present,
face to face, on cell phones and on face-book.
They have large support networks
and each feels free to travel anywhere at any time.
Their worlds are much larger than even
I can imagine.

Oldest Grandson's Wife- our first granddaughter
Amanda – mother of one little boy and twin girls.
Student, earning a Bachelor Degree -via the internet
Teacher-to-be
Viola, Kansas

The generations go on and on.
New ways of living
New ways of thinking
New ways of being
Always changing.

A woman's life is very different today.
The laundry that took a full day of toil
Is now done with the turning of a dial
every day of the week!
The iron is no longer heated on the stove
(if there is an iron at all)
Birth control helps women
choose when to be parents – or not.
Store bought foods
make the huge garden obsolete.
Dinners can come premade
in boxes and cans.
Take-outs exist.
Contacts are broad and freely available.

Women are in public places,
openly at work
in careers as well as jobs.
Women are filling many roles
including earning incomes.
Women feel free to travel widely
for work or for pleasure,
often driving while their husbands ride.
Fathers have learned they can
give baths,
change diapers,
prepare meals,
do the laundry,
and make the beds.
Yet often mothers feel overworked
and overextended.
Is more change needed?

Changes are everywhere
And they will continue.
Words cannot hold
the truth of it.
Women and men are
discovering new ways to be together,
sharing the roles and worlds that were so separate.
Both taking leadership in their homes,
communities, and their worlds.
We can never know where we are going.

Everybody Loves Raymond'
is a far cry from 'Father Knows Best'.
The world is being re-imaged in a fuller,
truer picture of today's living.
Men and women are depicted living side-by-side,
able to have differing opinions and disagreements,
each often openly bewildered by the other.
Even when married,
people may live more as intimate partners
than living prescribed roles of 'husband and wife'.
We see men and women
without many of the specific gender roles
of my earlier years.

My estranged paternal grandmother
worked toward obtaining
the 'right to vote' for women.
My maternal grandfather was noted for saying:
"The world went to hell in a hand basket
when women got the right to vote."
Women now take voting for granted
and think everyone considers it good.
Change happens regardless of the resistance
that afterwards may seem foolish.

My maternal great aunt
became an Osteopath
with her own practice in Oklahoma.
She was a never-married mother with a son

raised by her parents.
She, along with other women,
struggled to get the 'right'
to live independently and
enter various professions.
They were called 'feminists'
as if it were a dirty word.
Some women struggled to fill unexpected roles.
Now those roles are frequently expected.

Some say we are in a 'third wave' of feminism.
(First wave: women's voting rights;
second wave: employment rights)
In the perceived third wave,
women are re-defining, re-shaping, and re-forming
the worlds they live in and work in
to fit their identities and needs.
Whether differences are due to hormones,
genetics, nurture or nature;
changes and even re-formations are happening.

While working on my doctorate
at Boston University,
I conducted interviews with clergywomen.
I visited with a woman who was among
the early pioneer women preachers.
She was married to a clergyman.
She reported that when she began to preach
she knew she
'had to work twice as hard to be half as good'

as her husband.
Within a few days I interviewed
a young woman who was just starting out.
She asserted the many advantages
of her womanly gifts.
In two generations the tides had changed.

Can the 'Faith of our Fathers'
come to terms with the truth that
'Faith of our Mothers' is equally important.
In what ways do our religious systems
and our images of God need to change as
new generations arrive?
Can the changes be incorporated
into our present religious systems
with their focus on scriptures and traditions
or will the changes require
new religious systems?

I am concerned about those in traditional churches
trying to live according to tradition and history,
thinking that is the way to be
spiritually and religiously faithful.
Some try to enshrine
'the way it has been'.
Is there room for people
with new visions?
Can we adopt new images of God?

Writers are identifying this gender issue.
Brown, in the *DiVinci Code* writes about
the church's need for the feminine.
The popular book,
The Shack, by William P. Young,
depicts God as an African American woman
oddly named "Papa".
The movie 'Avatar' introduces
the 'Great Mother'
with compassionate connectivity
of everyone and everything
in 'Her' world.

Imaging God as female is obviously
not
just an idea that only two or three are considering.

The world is rapidly changing.
People have called our culture patriarchal,
but that seems to be fading.
Women have sometimes had a voice
in history,
but it was usually used in private.
Birth control, inventions, and new attitudes
have given women
time and energy
for public interests.
Television and internet
have given women around the world
opportunities to observe women
active in the public sphere.

Women are claiming
freedom to name their desires
and use their abilities
in ways that had been reserved for men.
Women *do* many of the things
previously done by men only.
This does not mean that women *are* men
or want to *be* men.
Most women are not seeking maleness.

What are we becoming?
It is different
than what we have been.
Life is like that.

Do established faith systems
have the courage and stamina
to pursue this question?
Do I?
Do You?
Do We?

Can we pray?

*God of life and love,
Mother (and Father) of us all,
guide us in this new venture.
Help us see one another
with new eyes.
Help us all live out of the core of our beings
Help us recognize your presence
within us.
Help us not be afraid to change,
to enter into a new day.
Help us claim the goodness
of the present time.
Open our eyes and ears
that we might see you
helping us find our way.
Give us confidence in new ways.
We turn to you for
motherly
love, wisdom, and guidance.
Please be with women and men
girls and boys,
giving us all assurance that
we are each created in your image
to share in the work and play that is before us.
Take away our fears,
our insecurities
and our anxieties.
We ask for abundant
living and loving.*

7. IS TODAY A NEW DAY?

*Today
is a new day.
Tomorrow
will be too.
Yesterday
has been*

*Today
carries yesterday
and leads to tomorrow.*

*Tomorrow
takes its reality
from today
and its tomorrow.*

*The present is not isolated
from the past
or from the future*

*What we do today
is critical.
It issues from yesterday.
It issues into tomorrow.*

*Today a new child
is born,
new ideas develop,
new technologies appear
Today matters-new happens
What we say and do today matters
Not only for now, but also for the future.*

Women are presently taking leadership roles
in many churches and denominations.
However, God continues to be
spoken of as male.
Women are still 'other than' God
according to expected and accepted
God-language.
It continues to be difficult to refrain
from expecting men to be 'more than' women.
It continues to be difficult to
refrain from expecting women
to be 'less than' men.
If not true in fact, then in pretense.

By the language used,
women and men have been encouraged
to identify men with God and
see women as 'other than' God.
Church history
re-enforces this view.
In Protestant religions,
the early protesters
removed Mother Mary
from worship services.
No longer were images of Mary
found in their sanctuaries.
Luther determined religious women should be mothers
raising their sons in the faith
rather than celibate nuns.

Roman Catholics and many other
denominations continue to
reserve leadership for men.
Popular interpretations of the Adam and Eve creation story
continue to encourage the image of
woman as a secondary 'helper'.
Mary Daly points out that many respected theologians,
including such notables as
Thomas Aquinas,
Martin Luther and
Karl Barth
affirmed that women are not
created in the image of God.
Many clergy have re-enforced these views.
This thought seems to have been present
early in Christianity.
The gospel of Thomas states that
Mary Magdalene would be changed into a male
so she could be part of the
kingdom of God.
The assumptions of men's superior position
has been everywhere
within Christian traditions.

Feminine images of God are
seldom named or recognized.
The idea of developing them
frequently seems like an
idea
better left alone.
Putting my head under a pillow,
going into a storm shelter,
hiding in the past,
all seem preferable at times.
However, changes happen.

As intelligent women (and men)
combine studies of gender, sociology, theology,
church history, and religion,
the constructed nature of our religions
becomes evident.
The **man**-made nature of our faith systems
is going to become more and more recognized,
and therefore challengeable.
New times are coming.
A hunger and thirst for naming God
with new feminine names
will become more and more apparent.
I can sense it.
My sensing suggests God wants this.
Is God tired of the male boxes
our faith systems have constructed?
I am.

The often history-bound nature of church
leads many people to believe traditions are of
ultimate importance.
To date most of our scripture translations,
our hymns,
our worship services
and conversations about God
continue to assume
the male language used for God is correct.
It comes out of at least
four thousand years of history.
The Holocaust has helped us see
history does not always reflect God's wishes.
People do have power.
We *can* question the goodness or 'God'-ness
of histories and traditions.

Some new hymn writers
are trying
to present and claim feminine images of God.
Some women working as
theologians in seminaries
are encouraging students to consider the possibilities.
Some clergy are minimalizing
the use of 'he' references to God
and using new labels in their trinitarian language.
I believe the conversation
needs to be openly taken to you,
the people.
Do we want to let the past fence us in?
Can we free ourselves to call God 'She'?
Can we help our daughters and sons realize
more complete images of God,
images inclusive of the female?

It makes me nervous.
What will the future be?
Calling 'God' 'She'
Could alter many things:
Self-perceptions
Religious practices
Ideas of 'truth'
Trinitarian thought
Liturgies
Hymns
Christianity
Patriarchal, non-Christian religions

Etc.
Etc.
Etc.

Is it safe to assume
words from Isaiah 43
can give us assurance
even in this discussion?
Are these words
written for us today
as well as for Israelites
in a challenging
and changing environment?
:
Do not fear
I have called you by name
You are mine
When you pass through the waters
I will be with you.
When you walk through fire
you shall not be burned.
You are precious in my sight
And I love you.
Do not fear
I am with you.

8. TRIPPING THROUGH MY 'RELIGIOUS' LIFE

I am constantly in the midst
of a trip
This way and that
Forward and back.
(and I have NO sense of direction)

Where have I been?
Who have I been?
Where am I?
Who am I?
Where am I going?
Who will I be?

How did I get into this?
I used to love
Singing my praises to
Father, Lord, and Him.
'He' was my bulwark.
'He' was my strength.

Why do I feel so different?
The previous balms now seem like
toxins of self-degradation.

Did I really think?
-or-
did traditions overpower?
Did I let the church
think for me?

Would a God that is pure love
want to elevate men above women?
In the past
I had so many answers for such questions.
Now none of them seem appropriate.
The old pieces no longer fit.

I taught church school, attended church,
went to bible studies,
worked on dinners and rummage sales.
Our children were raised in church
and church activities.
Then one day
I was delivering mail,
a man climbed in my car on a hot summer day.
He had a gun.
I stammered and stuttered.
I shook like a bowl full of Jell-O.
After driving to a remote spot,
I was instructed to stop.
I knew my life was finished.
I had been unable to get my mace.
My attempts to signal people were in vain.
I briefly thought of God
"God, it's just you and me".
Immediately my body turned.
With total confidence,
words streamed from my mouth.
"You are a child of God.
It doesn't matter what you have done.
God loves you and God cares about you.
Because God cares about you I do too."
His tears began. Shortly, he left the car.
Two days later he turned the gun on himself,
ending his difficult life.

I prayed for his soul.
The love I expressed to him
had affected the core of my being.
After three days of internal prayer
I saw a vision that set God's love
for the man in concrete.
My faith took on a new reality.
I had never considered such an immediate
relationship with God or the extent
of God's love for all people.
Eventually, I began to share the story
and later became a pastor.
I felt that the church was failing
to express the depths of love God has for each of us.
Whenever I heard "Jesus died for us"
I immediately thought "No, Jesus lived for us"
I began to feel a desire to re-form church.
I returned to school.

Sociology, psychology
scripture, church history, theology, spirituality.
It was an exciting time.
I didn't notice nearly all texts were written by men.
It was easy to ignore those by women.
I was again 'one of the guys'.
It was easy to critique women's writings
as frivolous and light-weight, unfocused and ambiguous.

A professor said: "you have to read Simone Weil".
She gave me a book about Simone's life
and it included some of her writings.
My eyes began to open.
This woman was intelligent!
This woman was insightful!
This woman was deep!
She seemed to know truths I knew
but had never put into words.
She found deep truths in everyday life.
She lived, assessed, and named her experiences.
This woman was spiritual and brilliant!
I painstakingly and voraciously read her writings.
I tried to follow her many levels of thinking.
She led me deeper
into my own thoughts and experiences.
She was extreme and passionate.
I respected her writings and her life.
I was excited by her determination.
She was an exception to my expectations.
I connected to her.

Later came Julian of Norwich.
I had vaguely heard about her.
I couldn't put her writings down.
It was as if she knew me
and was writing my innermost thoughts.
I wept.
What were those tears about?
I felt less alone.
Here was a famous woman writing
my spiritual biography!
How could she know the things she knew?
I still can't quite pin point the reasons
for the power of her writings in my life.

But again I connected
and was strengthened
as a spiritual theological woman.

My spirituality as a woman grew.
I began giving myself more freedom
to question the accepted church ways.
I discovered the writings of Catherine of Sienna
and other medieval religious women.
Eight hundred years ago they
raised up their voices.
They assumed the power to criticize
the established ways of their churches,
and their priests.
They criticized the focus on sin and death
(stressed to sell indulgences-
according to Catherine of Sienna).
They sought a focus on love and life.
These women wrote about their
mystical experiences as facts.
Much of their writing reflected
the teachings of the day,
but sometimes they thought for themselves.
They often wrote passionately,
speaking strongly of God's love
and their yearnings for God.
They were neither male priests
nor women busy with family life.
They were respected women who
exercised a public voice
because they claimed to speak for God
out of direct experiences of God's presence.
Amazingly, some of their writings were saved,
published, and read.

As a pastor
I became focused on Holy Communion
with its opportunities for
intimate experiences of God's love.
I did a major practical study
involving many laity.
I served on the denominational
task force to produce a document
on the subject.
I spoke out of my
experience.
Now I think I was expressing
my thoughts as a woman.
Perhaps I was gaining confidence
in my thinking
and speaking.

Later in my doctoral work at Boston University
I began to focus on clergywomen's preaching.
I was gifted with the richness
of their work.
I began to study women's ways.
I became aware of my own bias:
respect and admiration of women
and women's ways had **not** been part of my past.
I came to realize I had automatically considered
men's ways and voices more important and
better than my own
or those of other women.

9. WOMEN'S WAYS?

Ways?
Styles?
Tones?
World views?
Ideas?
Attitudes?
Carriage?
Assumptions?
Actions?
Voice?
Underpinnings?
All that and more?

What are women's ways?
Others have researched this question.
Others have published their findings.
Their research is broad
and based on direct studies
with many women.

No two women are the same,
and yet similarities and tendencies are uncovered.
Of course, men exhibit some of these,
but often they try to cover them up
for fear of seeming 'feminine' or 'weak'.
Weakness seems to have been associated
with women and their ways.
The academics who studied women
were **not** apologetic about their findings.
They seemed proud to be women
with women's tendencies!
They did not think women's ways were
less than men's ways.

At first I frequently wanted to
dismiss their findings
as pertaining to other women, not myself.
When I look back on that time
I wonder how I could have been so foolish.
How could I have thought
these 'ways' were examples
of weakness and inefficiency?

(Writings used for this section are included in the Bibliography)

Findings from **Carol Gilligan:**

Women were much more likely
to define themselves by their relationships,
while men usually defined themselves
by their accomplishments.
Women tended to value
connections and compassion,
caring, and intimacy.

They made moral judgments accordingly.
Women frequently found strength and power
in nurturing rather than in assertion or aggression.
(She wondered if men have been conditioned
or socialized to become other than this.)

Findings from **Deborah Tannen:**

She named women's proclivity to 'rapport'
and men's tendency to 'report'.
Rapport demonstrates the importance of intimacy,
connection, closeness, and community.
Rapport intimates the personal
and assumes the importance of appearing equal.
Reporting is more impersonal,
it assumes separation and independence.
Reporting displays knowledge and
assumes the goodness of hierarchy.
She refuses to identify one style as better.

Findings from **Carol Belenky, Mary Field, Blythe McVicker Clinchy, Nancy Rule Goldberger, and Jill Mattuck Tarule:**

They uncovered
women's inclusion of emotion and intuition and
the personalization of nearly everything.
Connection and closeness were important
in the development of women's 'voices'.
The connections included:
compassion, intimacy, empathy, etc.

Women expressed a desire to 'help',
and to 'make a difference'.
Women stressed understanding
in comparison to men's stress on strength.
The ear seemed of utmost importance,
stressing the importance of being heard in order to hear.
Men's practice of critical discourse and reasoned argument
seemed uncongenial for most women.
The women worried someone would get
'hurt' in the debate.
Truth seemed personal, particular,
and grounded in women's own experiences.
Women liked to share their ideas
and include personal stories and feelings.
Women used their voices more effectively
after they were aware they had been heard.
Women were encouraged when others said
they 'made a difference' or 'helped'.
A developed woman's 'voice'
uses reason to blend
her inner voice,
the expertise of others,
and her own observations and experiences.
It is rational *and* emotive;
contributing a blend of feelings *and* thoughts.
Women tend to be concerned about
inclusions and exclusions
and are aware of the feelings and lives of others.
Women's knowledge is grounded in everyday life
with tolerance for ambiguity, chaos,
contradiction, and complexity.

Findings from Nelle Morton:
She wrote of women's holistic voices.
A holistic voice integrates

theory and practice,
history and nature,
the personal and the political,
the body and the mind,
reason and emotion,
heart and head.
Women can listen better after knowing
someone has listened to them.
Women need to be heard
in order to become empowered;
Women use more
metaphor, intuition and imagination.
Women lose integrity
when they speak in the styles of men.
God is a Listening Ear who hears the heart.
Women are more likely to recognize
the value and uniqueness of each person
contradicting the present paternalistic attitudes
towards the poor and dispossessed.
Nelle Morton was convinced the survival of humankind
depends on the inclusion of women's holistic voices.

The characteristics noted by
these women who studied women's ways in depth
offered me new insights
into the importance and value of women
and women's ways.
This appeared especially true
when women feel free to be women
without needing to imitate men.
Their studies also opened my mind
to new previously impossible possibilities.
The leadership of women
in the public sphere
would undoubtedly bring with it

major changes,
especially
when women moved away from
imitation of men's ways
to acceptance of the goodness
of women's ways.

10. CLERGYWOMEN

*I visited a hospitalized child
his parents happened not to be there.
Later his mother reported this conversation:
"She was here!"
"Who was here?"
"You know, She was here"
"Who is She?"
"You know, Jesus was here."*

*Can we, like this child,
think of the divine as 'She'?
Is calling Jesus or God 'She'
'Wrong'?
This little boy assumed he was right.
My leadership brought this
confusion (?) of images.*

Two hundred Clergywomen
exposed their theologies and spiritualities
when they answered
my dissertation questions
regarding their images of preaching
and images of themselves as preachers.
Their extensive answers led me to consider the
very goodness of being a woman.
The following sums up my findings.

I share a few of their own words.
I personally connect with most of them.
(Reference to the dissertation is in the Bibliography -
participants agreed to an anonymous use of their words
in my future writings)

The **Spirit** was real and a continual active presence.
"When I am sitting down writing out ideas,
the Holy Spirit is the one who instructs me,
'this is what the people need to hear'".
"I rely on the Holy Spirit;
that is the only way I can walk into the pulpit,
to know it is not just me."

Love was one of the most used words.
They wanted to pass God's daily love
to the people and hoped the people would
do the same for others.
"My preaching is different
because of the centrality of love,
particularly God's love,
but also our love for each other"
Another writes simply:
"God is loving.
God is real.
God cares.
God wants to be connected"

The women wrote of a (w)**holistic** dimension.
One preacher summed it up:
"So often women say preaching takes all of them.
It's a different kind of sermon.
If God is calling women to do it women's way,
then we integrate
every single thing that comes along"

Listening is a prerequisite.
"This journey, preaching, is 90% listening
and 10% talking –
or maybe it's 99-1".
"People talk all week, pastor talks on Sunday.
Lots of listening is required."

Relationships are at the core.
"For me, ministry is about relationships,
with God through Jesus, and with the people.
Indeed life is about relationships."
"The hardest sermon is the first in a new appointment
where I don't know the people".

The word '**help**' took on significance
and a meaning indicating assistance with respect.
"I want to help individuals grow in their relationship with
God;
experience God's presence"
"I help people know they are
unique and precious in the sight of God",
"I want to be relevant,
preach what they need to hear,
help them reach their own conclusions
with the help of the Holy Spirit."

Heart and head were frequently linked.
These women often expressed the feeling
that the heart had been left out in the past.
"I came to believe that too much preaching is
head tripping and not enough heart touching"

One woman married to a clergyman wrote:
"My husband and I preach so differently,
it is as if preaching is **different**.
He is much more linear.
I'm more like,
picking up the diamond and turning it around."
Another clergy wrote:

"I turn it around, I change it, I reshape it,
I do this and I do that.

Clergywomen sometimes associated
their preaching work with **feeding.**
"A mother who loves her child
prepares healthy, appetizing food,
and presents it is an appealing way",
"My approach to preaching every Sunday
is to find new ways to offer real food
to God's people as I help them
connect their everyday lives with their faith."

Joys and burdens were linked hand in hand.
"I have a love-hate relationship with preaching,
finding it both a great joy and chronic burden".
"by Friday I panic,
Saturday noon I write notes
and do a lot of talking out loud to myself.
Sunday morning I feel sick that
I haven't fully prepared. But I am excited.
I LOVE preaching.
I enjoy the sermon while giving it,
but I berate myself all afternoon on Sunday.
The ambiguity seemed normal.

There was a strong focus on **life and love**
and very little reference to sin or death.
And yes, they frequently called God 'He'.
They may never have considered
the possibility of anything else.

Clergywomen's responses connected
not only with my own experiences,
but also with the scholars who had studied
women's ways.
Preaching was more rapport than report
A holistic voice was demonstrated
in their inclusion of
everyday life, experiences, studies,
thoughts, emotions. . .
Connections and relationships
were of utmost importance
and used to understand,
encourage, empower, and help.

Inevitably these clergywomen are defining God
to congregations by their ways.
God is Love and Spirit.
God's desire is for love to be extended.
God listens to us.
Every part of life is involved in spiritual lives;
nothing appears secular.
Relationships are critically important.
Thinking and feeling are intertwined and inseparable.
Listening with a desire to help becomes the core.

They are helping people
become more loving and caring.
This God seems much more interested in feeding people
than directing or judging them.
These clergywomen appear to be in the process of
transitioning into a religious system
focusing on encouraging people to
receive and share God's love and care.

Are these women defining a 'She' God
to their people
and yet continuing to call God 'He'?

In the midst of the research I started to realize
the richness of women's ways.
They gave words to many of my own experiences.
I developed respect and admiration
for clergywomen and for their ways.

In the beginning God created.
God creates yet today.
New worlds come into being.
New ideas sprout and grow.
New ways become appropriate.
New beginnings continually emerge.
Many women are leading.
Clergywomen offer a
God strong in:
love
spiritual presence

relationship

A God who:
listens to hearts,
helps and encourages,
knows and understands,
feeds and nourishes,

These clergywomen
want to share goodness
They want to help
people in their relationships.

Are 'sharing' and 'helping'
impotent weaknesses,
Or are they the greatest strengths?

These clergywomen did not express dissatisfaction
with male images of God in their writings.
The question was not asked.
I had never considered it myself,
not in 2001.

As congregations listen to women's preaching,
they are bound to develop
impressions of God.
As clergywomen continue to present their
images of God and God's ways
with confidence in their own 'women's' voices,
images of God are inevitably being altered.
Now it seems to me
the God named 'He'
takes on 'She" characteristics.
I am reminded of *The Shack*
with its female 'God' named Papa.

It seems so odd in the book.
Is this wise?
Is there another way?
Can we openly name God 'She'
As well as 'He'?

19.

On Mother's Days
I have frequently suggested that God
would not be offended if we called God Mother.
Perhaps God would not be offended
if we called 'Her' 'She' any day of the year.
This would not be only a linguistic change.
This would change the face of God.
It would add images of God.
Perhaps this is God's desire as well as mine.
Perhaps God wants to be imaged as 'She'
as deeply as 'He'.

Would God object to being called She?
We easily say mother nature
And mother earth
Can we call God Mother
Without dis-ease?
Can we imagine Her?
Can we hear Her voice?

11. ODES TO MY MENTORS

Where have the women been?
What roles have they played?
Women raised the children.
Women served the meals.
Did they do more?
Do we have religious role models?
Do we have records?
Who are they?
What did they think?
What did they do?
How did they live?
Are there traditions
we can raise up and claim?
Spiritually
Theologically
Religiously?

There are
Women I acknowledge
Women I love to portray
Women I feel I know intimately
My guides
My inspirations
My mentors
They have freed me to think
They have freed me to feel
They have given me permission
to speak and write and live.

**Ode to
Mary Magdalene**
I can smell the aroma
of the good news
the salve, the balm, the ointment.
I can feel your pain
at the death of Jesus.
I can hear your wailing.

Your work was just beginning.
You kept the good news alive.
You proclaimed the real continuing life of Jesus
You affected the lives of many
With your passionate love.

Were you the 'most loved'?
Did you lead?
Did your passion
surpass that of others?
Were you the first
preaching woman?

You have become a symbol for us
We seek you
We re-enact you
We feel your energy
We sense your passion
We know your extreme love
We imagine your proclamations
You live on in us.

Ode to the Woman at the Well
You came to draw water late in the day.
Were you avoiding the women who came early?
Did others make you uncomfortable?
You were so often dismissed by men,
married one moment, not the next.
Were you strong and opinionated?

Jesus spoke with you.
You spoke with Jesus.
He asked your help.
You conversed.
You asked him questions.
You engaged him
and found yourself exposed.
Jesus did not shun you.

You went and told!
You proclaimed Jesus!
You spoke.
People heard.
You convinced others.
People stopped what they were doing.
They took time to find Jesus.
You, who were looked down upon,
became the spokesperson!
You used your voice!

Ode to the Desert Women
Men moved into caves to seek God.
They fasted and sought holiness
in their loneliness and hunger.
You were not left behind.
You journeyed the same path.
You lived lives of solitude
and poverty.
Did you miss the world?
Did you stay awake nights?
Were you lonely?
Did you continue to serve the poor?
Is that what you were craving,
intimacy with God and people?
Did your yearnings find solace?
Did Jesus come near?
Did the hand of God stroke your hair?
Could you feel God's breath
in the wilderness?
Did your hungers bring
great spiritual feasts?
As your stomachs shriveled,
did your souls expand?

**Ode to
the Early Women who were Silenced**
You discovered something new.
You no longer had to sell your bodies
to feed yourselves and your children.
Followers gave you food and shelter
Did you sing, did you speak?
Did you lead?
Was it good to have a voice?
It didn't last long.
Men quieted you

Did they fear your reputations?
A movement led by women?
It would never do.
You had to be quiet.
Men took charge again.
They even hushed
the 'respectable' women.
Did followers of the 'way'
become followers of the men?

Ode to Early 'Religious' Women of the Medieval Era

Some of you lived together to
share your experiences,
to grow closer to God,
and to help those in need.
You were often educated
more thoroughly than other women,
sometimes by other women.
Some of you lived without husbands and children.
Some came to this 'religious' life after
husbands died and children were grown.
Some abandoned husbands and children.
Some of you lived in your homes
and gathered together during the day.
Your reputations spread
Others came
Your desire to draw near to God
and to serve God
attracted many.
Your desire to be educated and to educate
blessed many.
You changed lives.
You healed.

You provided light.
Young women came to you.
You encouraged their growth
into passionate caring God-loving women.
You challenged the status quo,
seeking better ways.
'Religious' women gained public voices.
You gained new identities.

Monasteries and Convents grew.
Organizations offered you new opportunities.
Some of you led numerous others.
Unencumbered by spouses and children,
you had time to study, pray, and work.
You yearned for and sought God
intimately.
You shared your experiences.
You did not follow the
expected ways of women.
. . .
Nearly a thousand years ago
Some of you gained a voice,
a bold strong voice,
a strong public voice.
You spoke for God.
You **wrote** for God.
You wrote about God,
a God of love and life,
a kind God desiring to heal and help.

You seem:
Strong
Confident
Insightful
Passionate
Intelligent
Educated
Energized
Spiritual
Bold

Yet you claimed to be
Small
Uneducated
Weak
Mere women!

You Wrote to Popes and leaders,
telling them what was wrong
with priests and churches and countries.
You encouraged spirituality and
closeness to God.
You encouraged lives of
service and humility.

You wrote to everyday people,
encouraging them to seek God's love,
assuring them of God's care,
blessing them with words of caring.

You dictated or wrote theologically and spiritually,
developing your own insights
from your learnings and your experiences.
You endeavored to record
your growing public voices.

Your writings
give us examples of women's
historical religious thoughts.
You were taught in traditional settings,
receiving the teachings of the church,
but you took energy and time to critique.
Your inclusion of the personal, emotional,
mystical, intuitive, and experiential
gives us a historical precedent
for the inclusion of these today.
You often claimed experiences of
visions and voices.
Some claimed
a God-inspired compulsion to write.

Passion is noted throughout your writings.
Your common thrust is love,
love from God,
love for God,
love for others.
For you, it seems God IS Love,
love leading to life.

**Ode to
Julian of Norwich (1343-1413)**
How did it happen?
How did you gain confidence
in your wisdom
and knowledge?
How did you gain respect?
Who were your mentors?
Were you scared to be enclosed,
unable to leave again,
a voluntary prisoner in and for the church?
So many came to listen,
so many came for your guidance.
I have been to your 'spot' in Norwich.
It doesn't seem spectacular.
How did you come to be published
when no other English woman was?
People sought you.
People listened to you.
Were you surprised?
Where did you find words and courage
to express your thoughts?
You defined God as Mother.
You opened this door for us.
You tried to uncover the meanings.
You guided the confused and troubled.
When all around you was troubling,

you helped people see that
all would be well.
You offered images of
God's tender comforting love
surrounding us as clothing,
wrapping and enfolding.
You claimed your visions
and interpretations as reality.
You inspire me, you feed me.
I wept when I first discovered your writings.
Your thoughts,
shelved for hundreds of years,
are alive again.

For you, God was so real
wanting the best for us,
reaching out to us,
loving us.
You shared God and yourself
with all who came by
Were you lonely
in your little room?
Did you have any idea
others were so intrigued
by you words and caring?
You proclaimed goodness
when all around saw disaster.
Where did you get
such assurance and confidence
in your thoughts and words?

Ode to
Catherine of Sienna(1347-1380)
Catherine**,** the name of my mother,
So many followed you

Popes listened to you
You criticized passionately
You stood up to priests who stressed sin and death,
to priests who lived immorally.
You acted passionately,
stressing God's grace, love, and healing.
You lived passionately,
catching Niccola's head at his execution
then refusing to wash away the holy blood stains.
You spoke and were heard.
You preached to crowds of eager listeners.
You wrote and were read.
You recorded your religious visions
and your interpretations.
You wrote numerous letters
to popes, priests, rulers, and everyday people.
You died so young,
33 years of age.
You inspire and encourage
me and many.

You had
a powerful energetic public voice
claiming
the truth of God's love,
living that truth,
the truth of God's
every-day, active love.
A gift from God to you,
a gift from you to us.
The light of your candle has lit many.
May I have your strength
to proclaim and live
out of my insights and visions.

Ode to
Hildegaard of Bingen, (1098-1179)
Brilliance beyond all measure
Leader and organizer
Reformer of church
Musician and composer
Healer
Scientist
Author
Preacher
You offer so many
refreshing and life giving insights.
Your connections with nature
lead to your acclamation of
moisture and greenness.
For you these were the
essential gifts.
I cannot approach your intelligence
You are an example beyond reach.
I read you with trepidation.
I can only struggle to know you.
You promise
God's intimate loving presence with
those who wash wounds with compassion
and treat simple, good-living people
with kindness.

Through your teachings we can pray:

God of abundant life
We are tired of dryness
We seek abundant life
Please give us your moisture
Please give us your greenness.
Let us sing the high notes
We will offer your salve.

You led so many women,
often educated by women

and living with women.
You developed theologies and spiritualities
that give life today.
Am I simply speaking and writing
a continuation
of the insights of women like yourself?

**Ode to
Susannah Wesley (1669-1742)**
Mother, educator, author, preacher,
philosopher, theologian.
'Mother of Methodism'
intelligent - educated – bold.
You gave birth to nineteen children
many of them died.
You went forward with power and strength.
You sought truth through
reason, studies, experiences,
and feelings as well as scripture and tradition.
Your excellent mind and heart
spoke not only through
your famous sons,
but also in your own life
and by your own pen.
You stood your ground,
had confidence in your thoughts,
expressed yourself -
even when at odds with your husband.
You taught God's
universal love and free grace for all
to your famous sons and to us.
You instructed and advised.
You encouraged the Methodist **zeal.**
You wrote and you spoke
your reflections and insights.

Ode to
Simone Weil (1909-1943)

Philosophy professor, political activist,
sociologist, moralist, theologian, author.
You were intense, extreme, and radical
in the way you lived and thought.
You were an intellectual spiritual giant.
You identified with the poor,
working in a factory and
dying refusing treatment and food
beyond that offered to a poor French woman.
You expressed strong convictions,
always seeking good for the downtrodden,
and you lived accordingly.
You wrote of deep hungers and thirsts.
You knew the suffering of extreme headaches.
You had no patience with condescension.
You were strangely authentic,
upholding your extravagant positions.
You, a born Jew, experienced and wrote about
times of divine presence
and possession by Jesus.
You learned Greek to pray "Our Father"
in its original form.
You came to see the gift of God's grace
and the rarity and miracle of real attention to God or another.
Grace and attention are evidence of God's love,
Suffering comes and is to be expected, like gravity.
Your writings excite my hunger
for the thoughts of intellectual, spiritual women.

12. VISIONS OF GOD?

Perhaps God is a quilter.
The quilter creates something warm and beautiful
out of bits and pieces of fabric,
using a variety of colors and designs.
The quilter takes things apart and puts them together again
creating something new, unpredictable, unique,
and perhaps never envisioned.
The quilter uses what is at hand
to create a blessing, sometimes planned,
sometimes created in the process.
You can see yourself as a piece of fabric
being used as part of the whole,
or you can envision the various times of life
as the fabrics and yourself as the end product.
Of course more will be added tomorrow
and the next day.
The quilt of our lives is ever changing.
Fabrics we would never chose
often add interest and character.

There can be many shapes and designs
as well as many fabrics in a quilt.
Each quilter has her own style
and way of being and doing.
The marks of the quilter
are everywhere on the quilt.
Hours of labor are required.
The results are always different,
yet in the end there is warmth and comfort.
When God is the quilter,
working internally and externally

Her marks are everywhere
creating beauty, warmth, and comfort.

Is God a mid-wife
encouraging us on,
even through pain and suffering
wisely helping us along
as we deliver
something new?

Is God a counselor
wise enough to ask helpful questions:
'What has happened?'
'Are you hurt?'
able to hear, guide, and respect?

Is God a masseuse
touching every ache and pain of life,
stretching us, healing our wounds,
using Her hands, Her salves, Her tones,
helping us become whole and well?

Is God a bread maker
using whatever ingredients available
to create goodness?
People who have been through
the most appalling times
can end up being a blessing.
God has the power to help a person
place a claim on all of her or his life,
without negating the problematic.
With God tending the dough of our lives,
all the ingredients blend together
until none is unaffected by the others
and the resultant life is greater than
any one of the incidents.
Just as a loaf of bread is made
from many ingredients,
some of them unpalatable by themselves,
God brings us to the person we are as She
develops and tends the dough.

One of my fondest childhood memories
is walking to my grandparent's house
a short way from home on Saturday afternoons.
There just might be fresh homemade bread.
It was made from the huge bags of flour.
The aroma, as we walked in, excited our innards.
Our mouths watered as we anticipated
the upcoming delight.
Sometimes we devoured a full loaf or two
fresh from the oven.
One year a teacher asked us to write about
a goodness in our lives.
I wrote about the bread.
Unknown to me, so did my cousin.
Bread is so simple and so plain.

We would never have eaten most of the
individual ingredients,
but treated with my Grandmother's skill
we had delicious tender bread.
It carried the love of a grandmother
along with nutritious and aromatic goodness.

Bread is frequently spoken of in religious life.
I have attended Jewish services
which ended with a sharing in bread and wine,
perhaps remembering the manna in the wilderness,
or the resultant 'bread of the presence'
historically kept in the holy of holies.
Many services for followers of Jesus end with
a service that shares bread and wine,
remembering the life of Jesus
and his declaration that he was the Bread of Life.
Bread, a basic food,
signifies 'life'.

In my work as a clergywoman,
one of the things I liked to do was make bread
in order to give people new understandings
of life and God.
We would talk about
our lives
in relationship to the ingredients.
Yeast to leaven;
unpalatable flour to fill and nourish;
liquid to bind and make palatable;
oil, that without other ingredients
would never blend with the liquid;
salt for a little taste,
sugar to sweeten.
Each ingredient could vary in kind and quantity.
We would add, mix, wait, add, mix, wait,
let rise, punch down, shape and let rise again,
bake, and eat.
At each step we would let our minds roam freely
sharing associated thoughts and experiences.

Rather than trying to ignore, cover up,
or cast out our everyday joys or troubles,
I tried to help the people see them
as part of the precious product.
I have never believed God
wants bad or painful things to happen,
but I have often noticed
life's troubles can bring compassion,
understanding, and new life.
In the making of the bread, my claim is,
with God as bread maker,
knowing us and the world intimately,
the loaf made from our lives
can provide food for us
and the world
using whatever ingredients are available.
This 'Bread theology' is holistic theology.
Perhaps it is a way to introduce a
more womanly image of God
in a non-threatening way.

What images of 'God'
come to your mind,
images that would offer theologies and spiritualities
more in tune with women's ways?
Perhaps you have wondered at
the strangeness of a loving God
who needs blood sacrifice
to release us from our shortcomings?
Did God need Jesus to die for us?
Perhaps rather than dying for our sins
Jesus lived, loved, cared, healed, and fed to bless us
and guide our ways and use of power.
Perhaps his death was then inevitable.

There are many ideas to contemplate,
once you give yourself permission
to question.
There are many more questions than answers.
Let yourself ponder.
Let yourself write
This section can go on and on.
These are only a few of my thoughts.

13. MESSAGES FROM GOD?

Can we hear God saying
??
Dearest children, sons and daughters,
My heart yearns for you
as only a mother's can.
I want to cradle you
in my loving arms.
I want to coo sweet blessings
into your ears.
When you only call me father
I become hidden
And unavailable to you.
Think of me as mother
I am tired of being hidden away.

I want to encourage you,
cheering for your every success
like a midwife during a delivery.
I am not your Lord or Master.
You do not need to obey me,
Listen instead to your
heart and soul,
to your body and mind
and you will detect me
helping and encouraging from within.
Think of me as your midwife
Helping you become your best.

My strength comes
from my integration with you.
My loving care

blended with your experiences,
feelings, thoughts, ideas,
and relationships.
These are the real life-changers.
Please do not shut me out,
absorb my attentive love and care
through the pores in your body and soul.
They will warm you,
they will help you,
they will cheer you on,
they will assure you,
they will guide you.
They will provide a balm for your
pains and sufferings.
They will calm your anxieties.
Salve-ation comes from this balm.
Think of me as a soothing salve,
eager to heal you.
Think of me as your most intimate partner
working, sitting, and playing side by side
with you.

You need not put your past behind you,
let it be blended with the present
let every goodness mingle with
the ever-present troubles.
If you will let me be the baker
I can feed you with marvelous bread
created from whatever ingredients I discover.
I can form you into a delightful loaf
for yourself and the world around you.
Think of me as a baker
Who can use the
available ingredients
to create something tasty and nutritious
for you and for others.

Let your life be whole
And you will be holy.
Do not forget or neglect

*the struggles.
Do not neglect or forget
the delights.
Let struggles and delights mingle.
Let me into your every
desire and thought.
I will help you live well.
Think of me as your helper,
eager to assist.
You have suffered.
You do not need to punish
or hurt others.
You do not need to punish
or hurt yourself.
Let me soothe your pain.
Know I am with you.
You do not suffer alone.
I have wept with you.
I can help you into the future.
Think of me as your physician
desiring to heal you.*

*Let me be your quilt-maker.
There are so many fabrics
in your life
so many textures,
so many colors,
so many patterns,
so many possibilities.
I am eager to choose some of each
and place them together
in special patterns and shapes.
I am eager
to create a unique quilt of beauty
using what you call drab along with the
brilliance of the stars;
using what you call darkness and light
and everything in between;
using the coarse and the smooth.
Think of me as quilt-maker*

*eager to create quilts of beauty and warmth
from your life, for your life
and for the world.*

*Take time to be,
to think, to ponder,
to create,
to notice the world around you,
to puzzle at the order,
to puzzle at the chaos.
Feel free to turn order into chaos
and chaos into order.
Creation comes from this.
Order and chaos are glorious gifts.
Think of me as loving co-creator
who basks in our new creations.
Take time for awe and wonder.
We come close during those moments
Life is beyond description
and beyond understanding.*

*You are alive!
Your dirty diapers were changed.
Someone fed you.
The world is all around you,
I come to you in it.
Live in the present,
knowing the past
has affected and shaped you
and others.
Live in the present
knowing the future will be born out of it.
Inhale.
Exhale.
Notice your breathing.
You are Alive!
Today!
Think of me as life-giver
Eager for you to breathe, and eat,
live and love!*

Talk to me.
Let me hear your thoughts.
Let me hear your joys.
Let me hear your concerns.
Tell me your deepest feelings.
Share your fears, your hopes, your dreams.
Let your soul speak.
Speak to me and speak to others.
As you speak
you can hear yourself,
you can grow out of your spoken words.
You can become more than you are.
Think of me as a listening ear
eager to hear you into fuller existence.

Think of me as grandmother.
Think of me as mother.
Think of me as sister.
Think of me as woman.
Think of me as she,
the one who wants to
hear you and help you;
the one who cheers for you
and encourages you.

Let my love and compassion
flow through you to others.
All have suffered, all need my salve.
Each person you meet is my child,
Notice them, respect them, care for them.
We are all one family
You are sisters and brothers
Interconnected to the world around you.
..
I yearn for you
Do you yearn for me?
Yearning has great power
Yearning diminishes the walls between us.

Yearning can bring new realities
There are many ways to live
Stay close to me,
I will help
I am a way-maker.

I Pray:

God,
I turn to you as Mother
Yet more than mother
Your love has nourished me
You have infused me.
You salve me with your balm.
You call to me in the night.
My soul yearns for moments
of knowing you.
Can I call you 'She'?
What language do I have?
The language of my past no longer fits.
Your She-ness seems so good.
There is Mother Earth
And Mother Nature,
Yet those names are not enough.
'God' still seems masculine to me
Goddess seems less than,
Sophia seems airy
I will call you
'She'
Can I?
Really?

14. AFTER-THOUGHTS

Does this bring us to a new place?
We are always on a journey somewhere.
These writings have helped me
sort out and concretize my thoughts.
You can write too.
…

What can we do or say
to help men and women on their way
to better relationships
and more accurate self-images?
Will we need to focus on 'God' as Mother
for a while to balance the thousands of years
of calling 'God' Father?
Today we create tomorrow's traditions.
We can make decisions for status quo
Or we can try something different.
I vote for something different.
I believe a decision for status quo
is a vote for the continued
overt and covert oppression of women
(and men),
the over deflation of girls and women
and over inflation of men and boys.
I believe a decision for status quo
is a vote to attempt to continue a
patriarchal church in a
non-patriarchal era.
I believe a decision for status quo
robs us all of
greater (w)holiness.
But I am not you.

You need to decide for yourselves.
There are no guarantees that calling God 'She'
will help women and men,
girls and boys.
There are no guarantees it
will improve relationships
or bring God-talk into a better and healthier place.
I believe it will.
...

Practically, what can we do?
There are little steps.
Use your ingenuity.
You can speak up when the theologies you hear
do not resonate with your experiences
of the divine.
Do not be surprised at resistance;
it is to be expected.
Ancient habits are hard to let go of.
Resistance does not have to shut us down.
We can persist.
In twenty years or so
others may hear us.

We need each other.
I hope these writings
encourage your writings
and group discussions.
More than that-
I hope these writings
inspire
girls and women (and boys and men)
to consider fuller images of God.

BIBLIOGRAPHIES

I am enclosing lists of articles and books that have contributed to my insights and reflections. These resources are often academic in nature but most can be understood by the general reader.

Women's Changing Roles:

Encyclopedia of Women and Gender. San Diego and London: Academic Press, 2001.

Particularly these articles:
Ens, Carolyne Zere and Ada Sinacore. "Feminist Theories" Vol. 1, pages 469-480.

Hamilton, Mykol. "Sex-Related Research" Vol. 2, pages 973-981.

Kravetz, Diane and Jeanne Maracek. "The Feminist Movement" Vol. 1, pages 457-468.

Lips, Hilary M. "Power: Social and Interpersonal Aspects". Vol. 2, pages 847-859.

Women's Ways:

Belenky, Mary Field, Blythe McVicker Clinchy, Nancy Rule Goldberger, Jill Mattuck Tarule. *Women's Ways of Knowing.* New York: Basic Books Inc. 1986.

Gilligan, Carol. *In a Different Voice: psychology theory and women's development.* Boston: Harvard University Press, 1993, first edition 1982.

Jordan, Judith V., Alexandra G. Kaplan, Jean Baker Miller, Irene P. Stiver, Janet L. Surrey. *Women's Growth in Connection.* New York, London.1991.

Helgesen, Sally. *The Female Advantage: Women's Ways of Leadership.* New York: Doubleday Currency, 1990.

Morton, Nelle. *The Journey Is Home.* Boston: Beacon Press, 1985.

Ruddick, Sara. "New Combinations: Learning from Virginia Woolf" in *Between Women.* C. Asher, L. DeSalvor, and S. Ruddick. Boston: Beacon Press, 1984.

Tannen, Deborah, ed. *Gender and Conversational Interaction.* New York, Oxford: Oxford University Press, 1993.
_____. *Gender and Discourse.* New York, Oxford: Oxford University Press, 1994.
_____. *Talking From 9-5.* New York: Avon Books, 1994.
_____. *You Just Don't Understand.* New York: Harper Collins, 1990.

Women's Voices-Theology/Spirituality

Catherine of Sienna. *The Dialogue.* (The Classics of Western Spirituality Series) Translated by Suzanne Noffke. New York, Ramsey, Toronto: Paulist Press. 1980.

Daly, Mary. *Beyond God the Father, Toward a Philosophy of Women's Liberation.* Boston: Beacon Press. 1973.
_____. *The Church and the Second Sex.* New York, Evanston, San Francisco, London: Harper & Row. 1968

Gottlieb, Lynn. *She Who Dwells Within: A Feminist Vision of Renewed Judaism.* San Francisco: Harper San Francisco. 1995.

Graham, Elaine. *Making the Difference: Gender, Personhood and Theology.* Minneapolis: Fortress Press. 1996

Green, Barbara Thorington. *Images of Preaching and the Preacher Held by United Methodist Clergywomen in the United States.* Unpublished Dissertation. 2004.

Hildegard of Bingen. *Scivias.*(The Classics of Western Spirituality Series) Translated by Mother Columba Hart and Jane Bishop. New York, Mahwah: Paulist Press. 1990.

Johnson, Elizabeth A. *She Who Is: The Mystery of God in Feminist Theological Discourse.* New York. The Crossroad Publishing Company. 2001.

Julian of Norwich. *Revelations of Divine Love.* Translated by Clifton Wolters. New York: Scholars Press. 1986.

Julian of Norwich. *Showings.* (The Classics of Western Spirituality). Translated by Edmund Colledge, O.S.A. and James Walsh, S.J. New York, Ramsey, Toronto: Paulist Press. 1978.

Kienzle, Beverly Mayne and Pamela J. Alder, editors. *Women Preachers and Prophets through Two Millennia of Christianity.* Berkeley: University of California Press. 1998.

LaCugna, Catherine Mowry, editor. *Freeing Theology: The Essentials of the Theology in Feminist Perspective.* San Francisco: HarperSanFrancisco. 1993.

Loades, Ann, editor. *Feminist theology: A Reader.* London: SPCK. 1990.

Mechthild of Magdeburg. *The Flowing Light of the Godhead* (The Classics of Western Spirituality Series) Translated by Frank Tobin. New York, Mahwah: Paulist Press. 1998.

Miles, Sian. *Simone Weil: An Anthology.* London Virago Press Ltd., 1986.

Oden, Amy, editor. *In Her Words: Women's Writings in the History of Christian Thought.* Nashville: Abingdon Press. 1994.

O'Driscoll, Mary, O.P. editor. *Catherine of Siena: Passion for the Truth Compassion for Humanity.* New York: New City Press. 1993.

Pagels, Elaine. *Beyond Belief.* New York: Random House. 2003.
_____. The Gnostic Gospels

Ruether, Rosemary Radford and Rosemary Skinner Keller, Editors. *In Our Own Voices.* San Francisco: HarperSanFrancisco. 1995

Teresa of Avila. *The Interior Castle.* Trans. by Kieran Kavanaugh and Othilio Rodriguez. Mahwah, N.J.: Paulist Press. 1979

Torjesen, Karen Jo. *When Women Were Priests.* San Francisco: HarperCollins, 1995.

Wallace, Charles Jr. *Susanna Wesley: The Complete Writings.* New York, Oxford: Oxford University Press. 1997.

Weil, Simone. *Gravity and Grace.* New York: Octagon Books, 1979.
_____. *Waiting On God.* London and Henley: Routledge & Kegan Paul, 1979; first edition 1951.

Made in the USA
Lexington, KY
09 February 2014